The Maltese Bichon: A faithful and loving companion

Author: Gonzalo Estrada

While every precaution has been taken in the preparation of this book, the publisher assumes no responsibility for errors or omissions, or for damages resulting from the use of the information contained herein.

THE MALTESE BICHON

First edition. March 14, 2024.

Copyright © 2024 Gonzalo Estrada.

ISBN: 979-8224337408

Written by Gonzalo Estrada.

Table of Contents

Content

Chapter 1: Origins and characteristics of the Maltese Bichon

Discover how this dog breed originated and learn about their physical and temperamental characteristics.

The Bichon Maltese is a small and charming dog breed that has captured the hearts of many people around the world. Its history dates back centuries, and its exact origin has been the subject of debate among experts. However, there are certain aspects that can be discerned with certainty.

This adorable canine companion is native to the Mediterranean, where it has existed for centuries. The breed is believed to descend from ancient companion dogs that were bred in the courts and palaces of ancient Rome and Greece. Maltese Bichon was prized for their delicate and elegant appearance, being considered authentic living jewels.

One of the most distinctive features of this breed is its long, silky coat, which gives it a majestic appearance. The hair of the Maltese Bichon is white, although sometimes it can have ivory or slightly golden hues. Your coat requires special care, such as frequent brushing and regular visits to the hairdresser to keep it in optimal condition.

In addition to its beautiful fur, the Maltese Bichon stands out for its compact size and its proportionate structure. His body is vigorous and agile, with a round, expressive head, and dark, bright eyes that reflect his intelligence and curiosity. His droopy ears, covered with soft tufts of hair, make him look even more charming.

In terms of its temperament, the Maltese Bichon is known for being a faithful and affectionate companion. They are affectionate and loyal dogs, who greatly enjoy human companionship. They love being in the spotlight and are very social, getting along well with adults, children and other pets.

Despite its small size, the Bichon Maltese is a courageous and energetic dog. They like to be active, although they adapt well to different types of homes. They are intelligent and endearing dogs, making them excellent options for owners who want to teach them tricks and commands.

The breed has a playful character and is always willing to participate in fun games with its family. They love to receive caresses and cuddles, and they enjoy long walks outdoors. However, they also adapt well to smaller spaces, such as apartments, as long as they receive adequate attention and exercise.

The Bichon Maltese has proven over time to be a loyal and affectionate companion for those who decide to share their lives with him. Its charm and sweetness are irresistible, making this breed a popular choice for pet owners around the world.

As a pet companion, the Bichon Maltese is a choice that won't let you down. Beyond its charming appearance, this breed has a balanced and friendly character that makes it the perfect companion for any home.

Although the Bichon Maltese enjoys the company of its owners, it is also an independent dog that can adapt to spending time alone. However, because of his affectionate nature, it is not advisable to leave him alone for extended periods, as he may feel anxious or depressed. These dogs benefit greatly from constant interaction with their family and the mental and physical encouragement this provides.

Despite its small size, the Bichon Maltese is an intelligent and energetic dog that requires daily exercise to maintain its health and well-being. Although your activity level may adapt to a more sedentary lifestyle, it's important to dedicate time to daily walks and interactive games to keep you happy and fit.

Early socialization is essential for the Bichon Maltese, as it will ensure that they feel comfortable in different situations and in the presence of other pets and people. Exposing him to a variety of stimuli as a puppy will help prevent undesirable behaviors, such as shyness or aggressiveness.

When it comes to caring for their long, silky hair, the Bichon Maltese requires special attention. In addition to regular brushing, it's important to take him to a trusted hairdresser to keep his coat in optimal condition. There, the proper cuts will be made and a professional bath and grooming will be performed. This type of care is necessary to prevent tangles and keep your coat healthy.

The Bichon Maltese is prone to certain health problems, such as eye diseases and skin allergies. It is important to watch for any signs of discomfort or discomfort and to take him to a trusted veterinarian for regular checkups and to keep him in perfect health.

In short, the Bichon Maltese is a faithful and affectionate companion, a dog breed that will steal your heart from the first moment. Its historical origin and its physical and temperamental characteristics make it an ideal choice for those looking for an affectionate and adaptable pet. With the proper care and dedication required, the Bichon Maltese will become a beloved member of your family and will provide you with years of unconditional love and companionship.

Always remember to give your Bichon Maltese the love, care and attention it deserves. Enjoy this wonderful furry companion and let your life be filled with joy with the presence of a Maltese Bichon by your side!

Chapter 2: Preparing to welcome a Bichon Maltese into your home

Maltese dogs are adorable and loyal dogs that provide companionship and joy to their owners. Before welcoming them into your home, it's important to take some precautions and make the necessary preparations to ensure that both you and your new furry friend are comfortable and happy. In this chapter, we'll give you tips on how to prepare your home and your daily routine to receive and properly care for a Bichon Maltese.

First, it's essential to condition your home to be a safe environment for your new furry companion. As small dogs, Maltese dogs are prone to domestic accidents, such as falling from tall furniture or the ingestion of small objects. Be sure to check every room and eliminate any potential hazards. Keep small items out of reach and place protections on stairs to prevent falls.

Also, consider the need to create a specific space for your Bichon Maltese. It can be a comfortable bed in a quiet corner of your house or even a small area bounded by a dog door. This place will be your personal haven where you can rest and relax. Make sure to equip it with toys, fresh water and a cozy bed to make it feel comfortable and safe.

In addition, it is essential to adapt your daily routine to meet the exercise and activity needs of your Bichon Maltese. Despite their small size, these dogs have energy and need physical activities to stay healthy and happy. Schedule daily walks where you can exercise and explore your environment. You can also include interactive games at home to stimulate his mind and keep him entertained.

We must not forget that Maltese Bichons are sociable and need to be in contact with their humans. If you have long working hours, consider hiring a dog walker or looking for the company of another animal while you're away. It's also important to establish a routine of quality time together, whether through walks, games, or petting and cuddling sessions. Remember that your Bichon Maltese craves your company and affection.

In addition, it is necessary to take into account the proper care of their characteristic fur. Maltese dogs have long, silky hair that requires regular brushing to avoid tangles and keep them healthy. Make sure you purchase the right brushes and hygiene products for your hair and consult a professional dog groomer for advice on how to care for and keep your coat in optimal condition.

These are just a few preliminary tips to prepare your home and your daily routine before welcoming a Bichon Maltese into your life. Remember that the arrival of a new member to the family requires dedication and commitment. In the second half of this chapter, we will share more practical tips on proper nutrition, socialization and training of the Bichon Maltese. Don't miss it! In the second half of this chapter, we'll continue to provide you with practical advice on how to properly welcome and care for a Bichon Maltese in your home.

One of the fundamental aspects to consider when receiving a Bichon Maltese is proper nutrition. These small dogs have specific nutritional needs and it's important to provide them with a balanced, quality diet. Consult your veterinarian to determine what type of food is most suitable for your pet and how much it should be given. Remember that Bichon Maltese are prone to dental health problems, so it's also important to offer them foods that promote oral hygiene, such as croquettes designed specifically for this purpose.

In addition to nutrition, socialization is a fundamental aspect of your Bichon Maltese's life. These dogs are sociable by nature and need to interact with other dogs and people to develop properly. Organize play dates with other friendly dogs and allow your Bichon Maltese to interact with people of different ages and characteristics. This will help strengthen their confidence, sociability and social skills.

When it comes to training, Maltese Bichons are intelligent and can be highly endearing. Spend time teaching him basic commands such as "sitting", "still" and "come here". Positively reinforce your successes with rewards and praise, and avoid the use of physical or emotional punishment. Remember that patience and consistency are key to successful training.

Another important aspect to consider is the hygiene and care of your Bichon Maltese's coat. These dogs require regular brushing to prevent their long, silky hair from getting tangled. It is advisable to brush them daily to keep their fur in good condition and prevent knots from forming. If you decide to take your Bichon Maltese to a professional dog groomer, be sure to establish a regular routine of visits to keep their coats well-groomed and avoid skin health problems.

Finally, don't forget to give your Bichon Maltese lots of love, attention and quality time. These dogs are loyal and loving companions who need to feel loved and appreciated. Spend time petting them, playing with them, and showing them your affection. Remember that your Bichon Maltese will be by your side for many years, providing you with unconditional company and unparalleled love.

In short, welcoming a Bichon Maltese into your home is a wonderful experience that requires specific preparation and care. Be sure to adapt your home and daily routine to ensure their safety and well-being. Provide adequate nutrition, socialize and train him in a positive way, take care of his fur and, above all, give him all the love and dedication he deserves. I am sure that this beautiful coexistence with your new furry friend will be a rewarding experience for both of you. Enjoy this special stage and create unforgettable memories with your Bichon Maltese.

Chapter 3: Food and nutrition of the Maltese Bichon

Proper care for our beloved Bichon Maltese includes paying attention to their food and nutrition. Providing him with a balanced and healthy diet is essential to keeping him in optimal health and well-being. In this chapter, you'll learn the right diet for your Bichon Maltese, from commercial food options to home-cooked meals.

Feeding our furry companions is a crucial aspect and we must ensure that they receive the nutrients they need to keep them active, energetic and healthy. To get started, consider that the Bichon Maltese is a small breed and has specific nutritional requirements. It is important to consider his size when selecting the right foods for him.

A common option for feeding our Bichon Maltese is commercial food, whether croquettes or wet food. There are several brands on the market that offer options specially formulated for small breeds like ours. These foods are designed to meet the specific nutritional needs of small sized dogs, providing the essential nutrients they need in the right amounts.

When choosing a commercial food, pay attention to the list of ingredients. opt for those that contain quality protein, such as chicken or fish, instead of meat by-products. Cereals, such as rice or corn, can also be part of the Bichon Maltese diet, but they must be accompanied by other, more nutritious ingredients and in balanced quantities.

If you decide to offer homemade food to your Bichon Maltese, you should keep in mind that this requires a little more time and effort, but it can be a healthy and satisfying option. When preparing home-cooked meals, it's essential to provide adequate variety, including lean protein such as chicken or turkey, red meat in moderate amounts, and fish rich in omega-3 fatty acids.

In addition to protein, remember to include a sufficient amount of vegetables and other fiber-rich foods to support your beloved companion's digestive health. Avoid adding condiments, salt or sugar to homemade preparations, as these ingredients can be harmful to the health of your Bichon Maltese.

It's important to remember that every dog is unique and may have different dietary needs. It's always recommended to consult a veterinarian before making significant changes to your pet's diet. Your veterinarian will be able to provide you with personalized guidance and specific recommendations to ensure an adequate and balanced diet.

In short, the nutrition and nutrition of the Maltese Bichon is a key aspect in their care. Whether opting for commercial foods or preparing home-cooked meals, we need to make sure they get all the nutrients they need to stay healthy. In the second half of this chapter, we'll explore more details about diet and nutrition specific to Bichon Maltese. Stay tuned for the next few pages and discover how to provide the best nutritional care for your furry companion!

In this second half of the chapter, we will delve into key aspects related to food and nutrition specific to the Maltese Bichon. Next, we'll explore the importance of adequate amounts of food, feeding schedules, and some useful tips to keep your furry companion healthy and happy.

Once you've decided what type of diet is best for your Bichon Maltese, it's important to pay attention to the correct portions of food. Although every dog is unique and may have different calorie requirements, it's essential to control the amount of food you provide to your pet. This will prevent weight problems and help keep your health in optimal condition.

Remember that Bichon Maltese are small dogs and therefore have smaller stomachs and metabolism. It's a good idea to divide your meal into several small portions throughout the day, rather than giving you a large amount of food all at once. This will avoid overloading your digestive system and promote better absorption of nutrients.

In addition to controlling food quantities, it is essential to establish regular feeding times for your Bichon Maltese. A fixed schedule will help regulate your digestion and prevent problems such as obesity or gastrointestinal disorders. Try to establish a daily routine that includes fixed times for meals, avoiding unnecessary variations.

A good practice is to provide him with constant access to clean, fresh water throughout the day. Bichon Maltese are prone to dehydration, especially in hot weather, so make sure they always have access to fresh water. In addition, if your Bichon Maltese consumes dry food, make sure it is always well hydrated, as processed food absorbs water from the body.

In addition to regular food, it's also important to give your Bichon Maltese a chance to enjoy healthy treats and snacks. These rewards should be given in moderation and never as a substitute for a balanced diet. opt for low-calorie, dental care-focused treats, such as special chews or chewing toys.

In short, to properly care for your Bichon Maltese, you must pay attention to various aspects related to their diet and nutrition. Controlling adequate amounts of food, establishing regular feeding times and providing healthy snacks are key practices that will help keep your furry companion in optimal health and well-being.

Remember, every Bichon Maltese is unique, so it's a good idea to check with your veterinarian for specific recommendations on your pet's food and nutrition. The vet will be able to provide you with personalized guidance taking into account the specific needs of your Bichon Maltese.

We hope that the advice and recommendations provided in this chapter have been useful to you to better understand the importance of food and nutrition in the life of your Bichon Maltese. Continue to give your furry companion your best and enjoy many years of love and companionship together!

Chapter 4: Care and maintenance of the Maltese Bichon's coat

By purchasing an adorable Bichon Maltese, you have become the proud owner of a faithful and loving companion. Their beautiful white coat is one of the most distinguishing features of this breed. It's important that you understand the necessary care it requires to keep it in optimal condition. In this chapter, you'll discover how to care for and maintain your Bichon Maltese's coat.

The Maltese Bichon's coat is plentiful and silky, giving your pet an elegant and charming appearance. To keep it healthy and shiny, you'll need to dedicate time and effort to its regular care. Let's start by talking about brushing.

Brushing is a fundamental part of caring for the Maltese Bichon's coat. You'll need to brush your dog at least two to three times a week to prevent knots and tangles from forming. Use a soft-bristled brush and carefully comb the fur, paying special attention to areas prone to tangling, such as the ears, neck and legs. This process will not only help keep the coat tangle-free, but it will also stimulate your pet's blood circulation and strengthen the bond between the two.

In addition to regular brushing, bathing is another essential part of caring for the Maltese Bichon's coat. Although you don't need to bathe him as often as other dogs, the ideal is to do it about once a month. Use a gentle, dog-friendly shampoo, making sure to rinse all of the fur thoroughly to remove any residue. After bathing, carefully dry your Bichon Maltese with a soft towel or hair dryer at a low temperature. Don't forget to pay attention to the ears and paws, as these are areas prone to moisture.

In addition to brushing and bathing, the coat of the Maltese Bichon also requires attention in other aspects. For example, spots on the coat are common in this breed due to rust and tears that can accumulate around the eyes. To keep the coat white and shiny, regularly clean the stains with special products recommended by your veterinarian.

Another important aspect in caring for the Maltese Bichon's coat is the frequency of cutting. Although some owners prefer to keep their fur long and fluffy, others opt for a shorter and more practical cut. Regardless of your choice, it's important to see an experienced dog groomer to maintain the desired style and ensure a safe and proper cut.

In short, caring for the Maltese Bichon's coat requires time, dedication and regular care. Frequent brushing, proper bathing, stain removal and proper cutting are essential to keeping your pet's coat in optimal condition. Remember that a proper care routine not only benefits the appearance of your Bichon Maltese, but also promotes their overall health and well-being.

**Below, I will provide you with more information about the care and maintenance of the Maltese Bichon's coat.

In addition to regular brushing and proper bathing, there are other special care you can provide to your Bichon Maltese to keep their coat in optimal condition. One of these practices is nail clipping. It's important to keep your pet's nails short and well-groomed to prevent them from getting stuck on objects and causing discomfort. If you don't feel comfortable doing it yourself, I recommend consulting a veterinarian or dog groomer to get them to do this task safely and properly.

Another area to consider is the dental hygiene of your Bichon Maltese. Many owners aren't aware of the importance of providing regular dental care for their pets, but this is critical to their overall health. Tartar and plaque build-up can cause oral problems, bad breath, and more serious illnesses. I suggest you brush your Bichon Maltese's teeth at least twice a week using a special toothpaste and brush for dogs. If you're not familiar with this practice, you can ask your vet to show you the right way to do it.

Eye care is also essential to keep the Maltese Bichon's coat in optimal condition. As they are prone to the accumulation of tears, it is important to regularly clean the area around the eyes to avoid spots and possible infections. You can use a mild cleaning solution and a cotton ball to gently clean the area. If you notice any persistent irritation or redness, I recommend consulting a veterinarian.

In addition to these cares, you must pay attention to the nutrition of your Bichon Maltese. A balanced, quality diet is essential to keep your coat healthy and shiny. Make sure you offer them foods that are appropriate for their age, size, and activity level. Consult your veterinarian for specific recommendations and follow the instructions regarding the amount of food you should provide daily.

Also, remember to provide your Bichon Maltese with a clean, parasite-free environment. Keep your rest area and toys clean, and check regularly for fleas and ticks. Always use antiparasitic products recommended by your veterinarian and follow the instructions carefully.

In conclusion, the care and maintenance of the Maltese Bichon's coat requires a regular care routine and dedication. It's not only important to maintain your elegant and charming appearance, but also to promote your overall health and well-being. Remember that each Bichon Maltese is unique, so you can adapt some of this care to the specific needs of your pet. Enjoy this experience and create a strong and loving bond with your faithful companion!

Chapter 5: Physical and Mental Exercise for the Maltese Bichon

Learn about this breed's exercise and mental stimulation needs and discover fun activities to share together.

The Bichon Maltese is a breed of dog known for its small size and silky white coat. Although they may live in small spaces such as apartments, it is essential to provide them with adequate physical and mental exercise to maintain their health and well-being.

First of all, it is important to note that the Bichon Maltese does not require an excessive amount of exercise. While they enjoy daily walks, they don't need long walks or intense activities. However, it's essential to meet your basic needs to maintain optimal physical fitness. Short daily walks, of approximately 20 to 30 minutes, are ideal for this breed. Make sure you wear it with a sturdy strap and enjoy a nice walk together.

In addition to physical exercise, the Bichon Maltese also needs mental stimulation to stay happy and satisfied. This breed is intelligent and enjoys mental challenges. You can keep your mind active through different activities that provide entertainment and enrichment.

One of the most popular options is to teach him new tricks. The Bichon Maltese is receptive to training and loves to receive attention and praise. You can teach him basic commands such as sitting, standing still, or standing up. Once you've mastered these commands, you can move on to more complex tricks such as going around, making turns, or even jumping low obstacles. Not only does training provide mental stimulation, it also strengthens the bond between you and your Bichon Maltese.

Interactive games are also great for keeping your Bichon Maltese engaged and entertained. You can use puzzle toys or prize dispensing toys, where your pet has to solve a challenge to get a reward. These games stimulate your intelligence and allow you to use your ingenuity to get the desired prize. Plus, they're a great way to keep him busy when you can't provide direct care.

Another way to provide mental stimulation is through exploratory walks. Instead of following a set route, allow your Bichon Maltese to follow its own pace and explore its environment. This will give you the chance to use your senses and discover new smells and interesting places. Remember to be patient as you walk, allowing him to sniff and enjoy his time outdoors.

In conclusion, physical and mental exercise are vital components to keeping a Bichon Maltese happy and healthy. Although they don't require a strenuous level of activity, it's essential to provide them with daily walks and adequate mental stimulation. Tricks, interactive games and exploratory walks are great ways to keep your Bichon Maltese busy and satisfied. Remember to adapt the level of exercise and stimulation to your pet's individual needs, always making sure they are comfortable and enjoying every moment together.

In order to avoid spoilers, we ended this chapter at an exciting and promising point. However, the next one is not to be missed, as we will explore some fun and creative activities that you can share with your Bichon Maltese. Get ready to discover a world full of games and fun in the company of your faithful and loving friend. Keep reading and be amazed at what's to come in the second part of this chapter! Continuing with our explorations about physical and mental exercise for the Bichon Maltese, in this second part of the chapter we will discover more fun and creative activities that you can share with your little furry friend.

An exciting option is the quest game. This activity stimulates both your mind and body, and natural instincts to seek and find. You can hide small prizes or toys around the house and encourage your Bichon Maltese to find them. Start with simple hiding places and gradually increase the difficulty. You'll see how much fun he has as he uses his sense of smell and sharpens his tracking skills. Remember to use healthy treats and limit the amount to keep your diet balanced.

Another activity you can try is socializing with other dogs. Bichon Maltese are known for being sociable dogs and they love the company of other canines. Organize meetings with friends or family members who have friendly, supervised dogs. Watch how your Bichon Maltese interacts and allow them to play and interact in a safe environment. In addition to providing, you with mental stimulation, this activity will promote your socialization and social skills.

If you want to challenge your Bichon Maltese even more, consider practicing agility. Agility is a canine sport that involves the dog crossing an obstacle course under the guidance and direction of the owner. These obstacles include jumps, walkways, tunnels, and others. Not only will you enjoy physical exercise, but it will also test your intelligence and ability to follow instructions. Remember that it's essential to use equipment and train with a professional to make sure they're doing the exercises safely.

In addition to these more specific activities, don't forget that free play is also essential for the well-being of your Bichon Maltese. Play throwing and looking for his favorite toy, make him run and jump in the garden or in a safe area, and let him simply enjoy his time with you. These moments of fun and joy will strengthen your bond and keep you happy and satisfied.

Remember to adapt activities to your pet's individual level and abilities. Some Bichon Maltese may be more enthusiastic about certain games than others, so find out what their preferences are and adapt to them. Also, consider your health and energy level before engaging in more intense activities.

We concluded this chapter at an exciting point, where you learned about the importance of physical and mental exercise for the well-being of your Bichon Maltese. I hope you have found inspiration in the different activities that we have presented to you, and that you begin to enjoy them together with your faithful and loving companion.

Remember that the relationship with your pet goes beyond exercise and mental stimulation. Give him love, attention and daily care, and your Bichon Maltese will reward you with an unparalleled friendship. I am sure that together they will experience exciting adventures and form precious memories.

Until next time! Read on and discover what's in store for us in the next chapters of this wonderful story of friendship and connection with the Maltese Bichon.

Chapter 6: Training and Socialization of the Maltese Bichon

Training and socialization are fundamental aspects for the development of a happy and balanced Maltese Bichon. In this chapter, we'll give you practical tips for training your precious companion and encouraging their socialization with other dogs and people. Let's get started!

The Maltese Bichon is known for its affable and friendly nature. However, like any dog, it requires proper education to learn the desired rules and behaviors. The first step in training your Bichon Maltese is to establish clear and positive communication.

Positive reinforcement is the key to motivating your little friend during training. Use rewards such as treats or verbal praise when your Bichon Maltese performs an action correctly. Remember that dogs learn best through gratification and positive reinforcement, which will strengthen the bonds between the two.

It is important to note that training must be constant and consistent. He spends time every day teaching new commands and reviewing the ones he has already learned before. Keep training sessions short and fun to avoid overwhelming your Bichon Maltese, as their attention can easily be dispersed.

When you start training your Bichon Maltese, start with basic commands such as "sitting", "still" and "come". These orders are essential to your safety and well-being, and will allow you to function properly in a variety of situations. Remember to be patient and persistent, as each dog learns at their own pace.

In addition to training, socialization also plays a vital role in your Bichon Maltese's life. Exposing him from an early age to different environments, people and dogs will help develop his confidence and sociability. Organize regular walks, visits to dog parks, and get-togethers with friends and their pets, always ensuring that these interactions are safe and positive.

During social interactions, watch your dog's reactions closely. If you notice signs of discomfort or stress, remove your Bichon Maltese from the situation and seek help from an animal behavior professional. Socialization must be gradual and respect the individual limits of each dog.

Remember that each Bichon Maltese is unique, so adapt training and socialization to the specific needs of your pet. By providing them with the tools they need to cope in different situations, you'll be helping your Bichon Maltese to become a safe, balanced and happy dog.

In the next chapter, we'll explore advanced training techniques and share valuable tips for addressing common challenges that may arise during this process. Don't miss the second part of this chapter, full of essential information for the growth of your Bichon Maltese! We will continue to guide you on the path to a harmonious relationship with your adored four-legged companion.

As you continue training and socializing with your Bichon Maltese, it's important to be aware of the challenges that may arise during this process. Each dog is unique and can have different needs and temperaments, so it's essential to adapt training techniques to your pet.

One of the common challenges during training is your Bichon Maltese's lack of attention or distraction. This breed tends to be curious and can easily disperse its attention to external stimuli. To handle this situation, it's a good idea to use attention commands and set clear limits from the start.

If your Bichon Maltese gets distracted during a training session, don't get frustrated. Instead, try getting their attention with a sound or a snap of your fingers. Once you've caught his attention, continue with the exercise and reward him when he performs the action correctly. With time and practice, your concentration level will improve.

Another challenge you may face is the aggressive or fearful behavior of your Bichon Maltese. This can be especially evident during social interactions. If you notice that your dog is showing signs of aggression or fear, it's crucial to address this situation appropriately.

First, avoid forcing your Bichon Maltese to interact with other dogs or people if it feels uncomfortable. Respect your limits and seek the help of an animal behavior professional if necessary. In addition, you can work on socialization gradually, starting with short, positive interactions, and gradually increasing the duration and intensity.

Positive reinforcement remains an essential tool during this process. When your Bichon Maltese behaves in a friendly and trusting manner, reward him with verbal praise and treats. These rewards reinforce the idea that social interactions are positive and rewarding.

In addition to regular training, spending time playing with your Bichon Maltese is crucial for their emotional and social well-being. The game not only provides them with entertainment, but it also strengthens the bond between you and your pet. Use interactive toys and participate in activities such as fetching and bringing. These games stimulate their mind and keep them physically active.

Remember that training and socialization are continuous processes throughout the life of your Bichon Maltese. As you grow and develop, you may need to keep learning new skills and facing different situations. Stay positive and patient, and enjoy every step of the way as you grow with your faithful companion.

With this information, we hope to have provided you with useful tips to train your Bichon Maltese and promote their socialization. Remember to adapt the techniques to your dog's individual needs and always seek professional help if you face significant challenges. Keep taking care of your Bichon Maltese and enjoy the wonderful company it provides!

Chapter 7: Health and veterinary care for the Maltese Bichon

Discover the most common diseases affecting this breed and learn how to keep your dog healthy through proper veterinary care.

The Maltese Bichon is a breed of dog known for its beauty, its white coat and its charming character. However, just like any other breed, Maltese people also have susceptibilities to certain diseases that can affect their health and well-being. In this chapter, we'll explore some of the most common diseases affecting this breed and provide you with information on how to prevent and treat them properly.

One of the most common health problems in Maltese Bichon is dental disease. Because of their small size, these dogs are prone to plaque and tartar build-up, which can lead to periodontal disease and tooth loss. It's essential to brush your Maltese's teeth regularly and schedule professional dental cleanings periodically to ensure good oral health.

Another common condition in this breed is skin allergies. Maltese dogs can develop allergies to different substances, such as pollen, dust mites or certain foods. These allergies can be manifested by itching, skin irritation, redness, and even hair loss. If you notice any of these signs in your dog, it's important to see your veterinarian for an accurate diagnosis and an appropriate treatment plan.

In addition, cherry eye syndrome is an eye condition that may be common in Maltese Bichon. It is characterized by inflammation of the lacrimal gland, causing a prominent, red bump in the corner of the eye.

While this may seem alarming, it's important that you don't try to treat it yourself and to seek veterinary care to evaluate treatment options.

Patellar luxation is another condition that can affect Maltese people. This condition refers to the displacement of the kneecap, which can cause lameness and pain in the hind limbs. If you notice that your Maltese is having difficulty walking or is showing signs of pain, it's crucial that you see your trusted veterinarian for a proper diagnosis and to establish a treatment plan.

These are just a few of the most common diseases that can affect Maltese Bichons. However, don't worry too much, because with the right veterinary care and constant attention, you can help keep your furry friend in good health.

Remember that prevention is essential. Scheduling regular veterinary visits, keeping vaccinations up to date and providing a balanced diet are key to the well-being of your Bichon Maltese. In addition, providing him with adequate exercise and stimulating play time will also contribute to his physical and mental health.

In the second part of this chapter, we will further explore specific veterinary care and recommendations for the Maltese Bichon. From feeding guidelines to tips for caring for your coat, we'll dive into everything you need to know to keep your Maltese happy and healthy. So read on and discover how you can be the best companion for your beloved Bichon Maltese. In this second part of the chapter, we are going to delve into specific veterinary care and recommendations for the Maltese Bichon, with the aim of keeping your furry friend happy and healthy.

Let's start by talking about food. A proper and balanced diet is essential for the good health of your Bichon Maltese. It is important to provide him with quality food, preferably formulated specifically for small and sensitive breed dogs. These foods are usually designed to meet the nutritional needs of Maltese people and can help prevent digestive problems and food allergies. Your veterinarian will be able to recommend the best option for your dog, taking into account their age, size and health status.

In addition to good nutrition, caring for the Maltese Bichon's coat also requires special attention. Their long, silky coat needs to be brushed frequently to prevent tangles and knots. It is recommended to brush it daily, using a soft brush and paying special attention to areas prone to forming knots, such as the ears and legs. If you don't feel comfortable doing it yourself, you can go to a professional dog groomer to give your coat the right care.

In addition to brushing, regular bathing is also important to keep your Maltese clean and healthy. However, you should be careful not to over wash it, as excessive bathing can remove natural oils from your skin, causing dryness and irritation. The ideal is to bathe him every two to three weeks, using a gentle and specific shampoo for dogs. Make sure to rinse it thoroughly to remove all soap residue and dry it completely to avoid skin problems.

In terms of physical activity, the Bichon Maltese is a small dog that adapts well to life in small spaces, such as apartments or houses without a yard. Although they don't need large spaces to run, it's important to provide them with enough daily exercise to keep their minds and bodies active. Regular walks, interactive games, and toys that encourage movement can help meet your exercise needs.

Last but not least, we must not forget about regular visits to the vet. Regular checkups will detect any health problems at an early stage and provide timely treatment. In addition to regular checkups, be sure to keep your vaccinations up to date and deworm your Maltese as recommended by your veterinarian.

In conclusion, maintaining the health and well-being of your Bichon Maltese requires constant care and adequate veterinary care. Through a balanced diet, coat care, adequate exercise and regular visits to the vet, you can ensure a long and happy life for your furry companion. Always remember to maintain an empathetic and loving attitude towards your

Maltese, because their well-being also depends on your dedication and unconditional love.

Chapter 8: The importance of play and fun for the Maltese Bichon

Play and fun are key elements in the life of our beloved Bichon Maltese. These activities not only provide entertainment for our furry companion, but they also play a fundamental role in their physical and emotional development. Throughout this chapter, we'll explore the importance of providing our Bichon with games and fun, so he can enjoy a full and happy life.

The Bichon Maltese is known for its energy and vitality, and play is a wonderful way to channel and harness that energy in a positive way. In addition to helping to release accumulated stress and tension, the game also contributes to strengthening the emotional bonds between the dog and its owner. By actively participating in playful activities, we generate a greater connection with our furry friend, which is essential for their emotional well-being.

However, it is important to note that not all games are suitable for our Bichon Maltese. We must ensure that we choose activities and toys that are safe and appropriate for their size and energy level. Search and recovery games can be especially beneficial in stimulating your mind and keeping you physically active, so it's important to select toys that are durable and sturdy.

Another aspect to consider is social interaction and play with other dogs. Bichon Maltese are sociable dogs by nature, and they really enjoy the company of other canines. Organizing play meetings with other trusted dogs can be a great way to provide our furry friend with an enriching and fun experience. This allows you to learn social skills, share moments of joy, and explore new interactions.

In addition to physical and social games, mental stimulation is also essential for the development of our Bichon Maltese. Interactive toys that challenge your ingenuity and cognitive abilities are a great choice for providing entertainment and stimulating your mind. For example, interactive food toys, where the dog must solve a puzzle to get his reward, can be a lot of fun and beneficial to his mental well-being.

In this first part of the chapter, we explored the importance of play and fun in the life of our Bichon Maltese. We have highlighted the need to select appropriate games and toys, as well as the importance of social interaction and mental stimulation. These activities not only help to keep our furry companion happy and healthy, but they also strengthen our relationship with him.

Continue reading the second part of this chapter to discover more interactive games and toys suitable for the Maltese Bichon! Don't miss out on the exciting options we'll present to you to keep your beloved canine companion active and entertained. Play and fun are essential in the life of our Bichon Maltese, get ready to enjoy unforgettable moments with him! An integral part of a Maltese Bichon's life is their ability to play and have fun. In the first half of this chapter, we have already explored the importance of play and fun for the physical and emotional well-being of our furry friend. Now, we'll continue to discover more interactive games and toys appropriate for the Maltese Bichon.

One of the toys that is often recommended for this breed is the plush toy. Bichon Maltese enjoy the softness and texture of stuffed animals, and spending time playing with them can be a great source of entertainment. In addition, these toys can also provide comfort and companionship when our dog feels lonely or anxious. It is important to ensure that the plush toy has no small parts that can come off and present a suffocation hazard.

String toys are another fun option for the Maltese Bichon. These dogs love to bite and pull objects, and rope toys provide them with an opportunity to satisfy this natural instinct in a safe way. When choosing a rope toy, it is essential to opt for one that is durable and resistant to the bites of our furry friend. Also, be sure to monitor the game to prevent it from swallowing chunks of rope or getting entangled in it.

Another toy that can be beneficial to the Maltese Bichon is the prize dispensing toy. These toys are designed to mentally stimulate our dog while providing him with a reward. The toy has compartments or mazes that the dog must solve to get its prize. This type of toy not only keeps our Bichon Maltese entertained, but it also challenges him mentally, helping him to develop his cognitive acuity.

In addition to toys, social interaction and games with other dogs are also essential in the life of a Maltese Bichon. Organizing play meetings with trusted dogs not only provides entertainment and fun, but it also encourages the learning of social skills and the development of good behavior. During these encounters, it is important to ensure a safe environment and to monitor the game to avoid any type of conflict or aggressive behavior.

Finally, we cannot forget the importance of playing time with us, their owners. Our Bichon Maltese seeks our attention and love, and spending quality time to play and have fun together strengthens our emotional bond. In addition, this gives us the opportunity to teach you new commands and tricks, providing you with additional enrichment.

In short, play and fun are essential elements in the life of our Bichon Maltese. Throughout this chapter, we have explored different options for games and toys suitable to meet your physical, mental and social needs. Remember to choose games and toys that are safe, durable, and appropriate for your size and energy. In addition, take advantage of these fun moments to strengthen your relationship with your furry companion. Enjoy every moment of play and fun with your Bichon Maltese, creating unforgettable memories together!

Chapter 9: How to Stress-Free Travel with Your Bichon Maltese

L earn techniques and tips for traveling safely and stress-free with your faithful furry companion.

Traveling is an exciting experience for many people, but when you have a Bichon Maltese as a faithful companion, there can be some concern about how to do it safely and stress-free for both of you. Fortunately, there are techniques and tips that can make your trips an enjoyable and hassle-free experience.

Before embarking on any trip with your Bichon Maltese, it is important to prepare it properly. A visit to the vet to ensure that your furry friend is in good health and has all his vaccines up to date is essential. In addition, if you are planning to travel by plane, you need to check the airline's requirements for documentation and transportation of pets.

Once you've prepared your Bichon Maltese for the trip, it's time to consider the mode of transport you'll use. If you're traveling by car, it's important to make sure your pet is traveling safely in the vehicle. You can choose to use a carrying cage or a safety harness specifically designed for dogs. This way, your faithful companion will be protected in the event of sudden braking or an accident.

During the car trip, it's essential to make regular stops to allow your Bichon Maltese to stretch its legs and relieve itself. Bringing fresh water and some treats to reward you for behaving well along the way can also be helpful. Also, avoid leaving it alone in the car, especially on hot days, as high temperatures can be dangerous for dogs.

If your plan is to travel by plane, it's important to research the airline's regulations and policies ahead of time. Some airlines allow small sized dogs to travel in the cabin, as long as they meet certain size and transportation requirements. Another important detail is to make sure that your Bichon Maltese is comfortable in its transport cage, providing it with a blanket or small pillow to make it feel safe.

No matter what mode of transport you choose, it's essential that your Bichon Maltese feels comfortable and safe during the trip. This involves creating a family atmosphere in your rest area, carrying your favorite toys or a blanket with your scent to calm you down during the journey. You can even play relaxing dog music, which can help create a calming atmosphere.

In conclusion, traveling with your Bichon Maltese can be a wonderful experience if you take the necessary precautions. Preparing your furry friend properly, choosing the right mode of transport and creating a safe and comfortable environment are key factors for stress-free travel. Remember that the happiness and well-being of your faithful companion should always be your primary concern during the trip.

Once you've taken all the necessary precautions to travel safely and stress-free with your Bichon Maltese, it's time to dive into the second part of this chapter and address some additional recommendations that will be of great help during your trip.

During the journey, it's important to ensure that your faithful companion is comfortable and safe at all times. If you're traveling by car, you might consider using a soft blanket or pillow so you can rest and relax during your trip. You can also take some of his favorite toys with you to provide him with entertainment and distraction.

If, on the other hand, you've chosen to travel by plane, it's important to note that flight conditions can be stressful for your pet. Therefore, it is recommended that you keep it in its closed transport cage and in a safe place at all times. In addition, it is essential to follow the instructions of the airline staff regarding the handling and location of your Bichon Maltese during the flight.

During the trip, it's essential to pay attention to your pet's basic needs. Make sure you bring enough fresh water to keep her hydrated and to schedule regular stops so she can stretch her legs and relieve herself. Also, be sure to carry a small bag with you to collect your waste and keep the environment clean during the trip.

Another important aspect to consider is how to feed your Bichon Maltese during the trip. It is recommended that you avoid giving him large or heavy food just before starting the trip, as this can cause an upset stomach. Choose to feed him lightly before leaving and take some prizes or treats with you that can be used as a reward along the way.

When it comes to safety while traveling, it's essential to remember that your Bichon Maltese must always be restrained and secure in its designated place. Use a safety harness or suitable transport cage to prevent you from escaping or getting hurt in the event of sudden braking or an accident. Remember that the safety of your faithful companion is your responsibility and you must take all necessary steps to ensure it.

Finally, it's important to keep a calm and positive attitude while traveling. Dogs, like humans, can sense the emotions and mood of their owners, so if you find yourself stressed or anxious, your pet is likely to be stressed out as well. Stay calm, speak in a soft and affectionate voice, and provide your Bichon Maltese with the security and peace of mind it needs during the trip.

In conclusion, traveling with your Bichon Maltese can be a wonderful experience if you follow some tips and recommendations. Avoid stress and worry by preparing it properly, choosing the right means of transport and ensuring your comfort and safety at all times. Remember that your pet is part of your family and their happiness and well-being are paramount during the trip. Enjoy this experience with your faithful companion and create unforgettable memories together.

Chapter 10: The Maltese Bichon as a therapy and assistance dog

Learn how the Bichon Maltese can play an important role as a therapy and assistance dog, providing companionship and support to people in need.

Known for its affable character and charming appearance, the Bichon Maltese has proven to be a faithful and affectionate companion for many people in its role as a therapy and assistance dog. Over the years, his dedication and special abilities have made him a true four-legged hero.

When it comes to providing emotional support, Maltese Bichons are true experts. Their caring nature and innate ability to understand human emotions make them ideal companions for people going through difficult times or suffering from medical conditions that require emotional assistance.

In the context of therapy, the Bichon Maltese plays a crucial role in providing comfort to individuals struggling with emotional problems such as anxiety, depression or stress. Its presence in therapeutic settings, such as hospitals or rehabilitation centers, has proven to have a positive impact on the recovery and well-being of patients.

Pet owners who have experienced the healing power of a Maltese Bichon highlight its ability to relieve stress and promote relaxation. Caressing their soft white fur and enjoying their calm presence can create a sense of calm and well-being in those who find themselves in difficult situations. It's no wonder that many therapists recommend it as an additional tool in their therapy sessions.

But the Bichon Maltese not only stands out in the field of emotional therapy, it has also demonstrated impressive abilities in the field of care. His intelligence and ability to learn specific tasks make him an ideal candidate to work as an assistance dog.

In situations where there are people with physical disabilities, the Bichon Maltese can be trained to perform specific tasks, such as bringing objects, opening doors or even helping those who have mobility difficulties to get up. Its small size and physical shape make it easily manageable in domestic environments or in small spaces,

WHICH MAKES IT AN IDEAL option for people who require constant assistance in their daily lives.

But perhaps the most impactful thing about the Maltese Bichon's role as an assistance dog is its ability to detect and alert its owners to medical conditions. Numerous cases have been reported in which these little furry animals have been able to detect subtle changes in the health of their owners, such as sudden drops in sugar in people with diabetes or even the presence of tumors.

The second half of this chapter will reveal even more about the impressive abilities of the Maltese Bichon as a therapy and assistance dog. We will explore real cases and learn moving stories of how these caring companions have changed the lives of many people. Don't miss it!

In this second half of the chapter, we will continue to discover the impressive abilities of the Maltese Bichon as a therapy and assistance dog, through real cases and moving stories of how these loving companions have changed the lives of many people in need.

One of the areas in which the Bichon Maltese has proven to be especially talented is in therapy for children with special needs. Their friendly nature and willingness to adapt to various situations make them ideal companions for children with autism, autism spectrum disorders, or other special conditions. Their comforting presence can help these children feel safe and comfortable, and their participation in therapy activities can encourage interaction and the development of social skills.

There are numerous reports of children who have found in the Bichon Maltese a faithful and loyal friend, able to understand their needs and provide them with emotional support. These furry little ones have become trusted companions in language therapy, occupational therapy and other forms of therapeutic intervention, making it easier for children to participate and progress in these activities.

In addition, the Bichon Maltese has also proven to be an excellent assistance dog for the elderly. This furry companion can provide a constant and comforting presence for those who live alone or who have mobility difficulties. These dogs can learn specific tasks according to the needs of each person, such as remembering to take medication, looking for lost items or even alerting in the event of an emergency.

For many older people, having a Bichon Maltese as a caring companion can make the difference between an independent and dependent life. These small dogs are capable of providing company, joy and security, alleviating the feeling of loneliness and promoting greater autonomy.

We cannot overlook the incredible ability of the Maltese Bichon to detect and alert to medical conditions. In numerous cases, these dogs have proven to be able to detect subtle changes or health problems in their owners, such as the presence of diseases such as cancer, epilepsy or allergies.

This amazing ability is believed to be due to their keen sense of smell, which gives them the ability to detect chemical changes in the human body. Early detection of these medical conditions can allow for earlier and more effective treatment, potentially saving lives.

In conclusion, the Bichon Maltese has earned its place as an exceptional therapy and assistance dog. Their affable character, their capacity for emotional understanding and their willingness to learn specific tasks make this breed an ideal choice for providing companionship and support to people in need.

In the second half of this chapter, we explored how these furry little ones are able to help children with special needs therapy, provide support to older people and alert them to medical conditions. Their moving stories and their positive impact on people's lives show us why the Bichon Maltese is a faithful and loving companion in the field of therapy and care.

Don't miss the second half of this chapter, where we'll continue to discover more about the incredible world of the Maltese Bichon as a therapy and assistance dog!

Chapter 11: The Bichon Maltese in the family

Learn how to integrate the Bichon Maltese into the family dynamic and develop strong and lasting bonds with each member of the family.

The Bichon Maltese is a small dog breed known for its gentleness and affection. Its compact size, white coat and angelic face make this breed a popular choice for those looking for a faithful and loving companion in the home. But how to integrate this little one into the family dynamic? Here are some tips for strengthening those ties.

The first thing to keep in mind is that the Bichon Maltese is an extremely sociable dog and craves human companionship. Therefore, it's crucial to ensure that every member of the family devotes time and attention to it. This means not only petting and playing with him, but also involving him in daily activities. You can assign specific tasks to each member of the family, such as taking care of their diet, taking care of their fur or daily walks. In this way, individual bonds will be established between the Bichon Maltese and each member of the family, thus promoting their relationship.

In addition, it is important to remember that the character of the Maltese Bichon is cheerful and playful. This breed enjoys interactive games, both indoors and outdoors. Providing him with suitable toys and spending time to play together will strengthen the bond between the Bichon Maltese and the family. Make sure the games are safe and appropriate for their size and energy level.

Another fundamental aspect of integrating the Bichon Maltese into the family dynamic is to provide them with their own space in the home. You can create an area where the dog has his bed, toys and his belongings. This will give you a sense of belonging and security, and it will also teach you to respect your own space and to have some independence. Teach him to come to his area when he needs to rest or be calm, so he will feel comfortable and an integral part of the family.

However, don't forget to involve your Bichon Maltese in family activities outside the home. Walks to the park, family outings, or simply spending time together outdoors can be enriching experiences for everyone. During these outings, be sure to keep your dog safe and protected, using an appropriate collar and leash and paying attention to their needs and reactions.

In short, integrating the Bichon Maltese into the family dynamic involves dedicating time and attention from all members of the family. By including it in daily activities, providing it with its own space and participating in interactive games, you'll be building strong and lasting bonds with your canine companion. Remember that the relationship with your Bichon Maltese is a mutual commitment, and as you progress in your coexistence with him, the second chapter of this chapter will reveal even more tips to consolidate this beautiful relationship.

As you continue to strengthen the relationship with your Bichon Maltese, it's important to remember that clear and effective communication is key to harmonious living together. Although dogs can't speak our language, they are able to understand our emotions and body signals. Use a calm, loving tone of voice when interacting with your pet, and be consistent in your commands and commands. This will help your Bichon Maltese understand what you expect from him and feel secure in his role in the family.

Socialization is also a fundamental aspect in the life of a Maltese Bichon. Exposing him to different people, animals and environments from an early age will allow him to feel comfortable in new situations and avoid developing unwanted behaviors, such as shyness or aggressiveness. Organize meetings with friends or family and their pets, or take him to dog parks where he can interact with other dogs in a controlled and safe way. This will help build their confidence and sociability.

Remember that proper training is essential for a well-behaved Bichon Maltese. Invest time teaching him basic commands such as "sitting", "still" or "come here". Use positive rewards, such as treats or verbal praise, to reinforce their good behavior. Be patient and consistent in your teaching, and you will see how your Bichon Maltese becomes an obedient and reliable dog.

In addition to the practical aspects of family, it's just as important to provide your Bichon Maltese with constant love and affection. Spending time to caress him, hug him and show him your affection will strengthen the emotional bond between the two and make him feel loved and valued. The Bichon Maltese is a companion dog par excellence and enjoys being close to their loved ones.

Last but not least, don't forget to take care of the health and well-being of your Bichon Maltese. It provides a balanced diet appropriate to your needs, as well as a regular exercise program. Keep his vaccines and vet visits up to date, and be sure to keep him free of parasites and diseases. Caring for your pet responsibly will ensure its happiness and longevity.

In conclusion, integrating the Bichon Maltese into the family dynamic not only involves dedicating time and attention, but also setting clear limits and encouraging effective communication. Socialization, training and proper care are essential aspects for a harmonious coexistence and a strong and lasting relationship with your Bichon Maltese. As you apply these tips and continue to nurture the bond with your furry companion, you'll find special joy in having a Bichon Maltese as part of your family.

End.

Chapter 12: Essential toys and accessories for your Maltese Dog

Discover the toys and accessories that cannot be missing in your Bichon Maltese's life to keep him entertained and happy.

We all love watching our adorable Maltese Bichon playing and having fun. They are little companions of life that fill our days with joy and tenderness. To ensure their well-being and happiness, it is essential to provide them with a variety of toys and accessories that fit their needs.

The first toy that cannot be missing in your Bichon Maltese's life is a soft and resistant ball. These dogs love to play chasing and catching objects, and a ball is the perfect toy to satisfy their hunting instincts. Choose an appropriately sized ball for your Bichon Maltese and make sure it's durable to withstand bites and vigorous play.

In addition to the ball, chew toys are essential for keeping your Bichon Maltese entertained and satisfying its natural need to bite. opt for toys made specifically for dogs, which are resistant and safe for their health. Cord or rubber chewable toys are great options, helping to clean your Bichon Maltese's teeth while playing.

Another essential accessory for your Bichon Maltese is a suitable feeder and drinker. These adorable dogs need constant access to fresh, clean water, so a quality drinking fountain is essential. In addition, the feeder must be suitable for its size and height, which will help prevent digestive problems and maintain proper posture during feeding.

In addition to the toys and accessories mentioned above, it is important to provide your Bichon Maltese with a comfortable and cozy bed. These dogs are known for their love of comfort and rest, so a soft, appropriately sized bed is essential to their well-being. You can opt for an orthopedic bed, especially if your Bichon Maltese is older or has joint problems.

To satisfy their curiosity and stimulate their mind, don't forget to include interactive toys in the life of your Bichon Maltese. These challenging and fun toys provide entertainment and help keep your pet mentally active. Toys with prize or puzzle dispensers are great options to boost your intelligence and keep you entertained for hours.

Remember that every Bichon Maltese is unique and may have different preferences when it comes to toys and accessories. Observe their behavior and discover what kind of toys they find most interesting and entertaining. By providing them with the right toys and accessories, you'll be helping to keep them happy, stimulated and healthy.

In the second part of this chapter, we'll explore more essential toys and accessories that will make your Bichon Maltese's life even more exciting. Get ready to discover new options and surprises to pamper your faithful four-legged friend! For now, enjoy watching your Bichon Maltese have fun with the toys and accessories he already has at his disposal. The fun is just beginning.

It will continue... During the second part of this chapter, we will delve into more essential toy and accessory options to keep your Bichon Maltese happy and entertained. We'll explore some options that can add even more fun to the life of your little four-legged companion.

One of the toys that cannot be missing in your Bichon Maltese's life is an interactive toy that stimulates their intelligence. These challenging toys are a great way to keep your pet mentally active and avoid boredom. An example of this type of toy is a prize dispensing ball. These balls with openings allow your Bichon Maltese to play to push it and receive prizes from the inside. In addition to keeping you entertained, they also help you develop cognitive skills through play.

Another essential accessory for your Bichon Maltese is a quality necklace and strap. These small, energetic dogs need to go for regular walks to exercise and socialize. A comfortable and sturdy collar, together with an appropriate length strap, will allow you to have greater control over your pet during walks. Make sure you choose an adjustable collar that fits your Bichon Maltese's neck perfectly, and a strap that's lightweight yet sturdy.

It is also important to mention the importance of interactive toys for the dental care of your Bichon Maltese. These toys are designed to clean your pet's teeth and massage your pet's gums while playing. Opt for rubber toys with special textures or toothbrushes for dogs to keep your Bichon Maltese's oral health in optimal condition.

As for grooming accessories, one of the essential options is a brush or comb suitable for the coat of the Maltese Bichon. These dogs tend to have long, silky coats that require regular care. A soft-bristled brush, specially designed for dogs with long coats, will help you to untangle the knots and keep your Bichon Maltese's coat in good condition. In addition, you can also consider having a specific shampoo for this breed, which will help keep their coat clean and shiny.

Last but not least, a soft and cozy plush toy can be a perfect complement to your Bichon Maltese. These dogs love having something soft and fluffy to cuddle up with, especially during rest hours. A plush toy can also act as a comforting companion for your pet when it's home alone.

Remember that every Bichon Maltese is unique and may have different preferences for toys and accessories. It is important to observe his behavior and find out which toys are the most attractive and fun for him. By providing them with the right toys and accessories, you'll be helping to keep your Bichon Maltese happy, stimulated and healthy.

As you continue to discover new options and surprises to pamper your faithful four-legged friend, you'll find that the fun is just beginning. Keep exploring and make the most of the companionship and joy that your Bichon Maltese brings you every day.

Don't miss the next chapter, where we'll explore more ways to enrich the life of your Bichon Maltese and strengthen your bond even more! More exciting adventures await you with your loyal and loving companion!

Chapter 13: How to teach your Bichon Maltese fun tricks

The Bichon Maltese, a breed known for its elegance and sweetness, can become a loyal and loving companion in your home. In addition to being an excellent pet, it is also possible to teach him fun tricks that will impress everyone. In this chapter, you'll learn training techniques to achieve this.

To teach your Bichon Maltese fun tricks, it's essential to establish clear and affectionate communication with him. The bond between you and your pet is essential for the learning process to be successful. Remember that every dog learns at their own pace, so be patient and enjoy the process.

Before starting with the tricks, it is important that your Bichon Maltese has previously acquired some basic commands, such as "sitting" and "still". These basic commands lay the foundation for learning more complex tricks.

The first fun trick you can teach your Bichon Maltese is to "screw up". To do this, start by holding a small reward in your closed hand. Then move it closer to your nose so you can smell it. While holding the treat, clearly say the command "leg" and raise your hand slightly, encouraging him to stretch his paw towards you. The moment your Bichon Maltese touches your hand with its paw, congratulate him and give him the reward. Repeat this process several times until you can do it without the help of the reward.

The next fun trick you can teach him is to "turn". Start by giving the command "turn" as you gently guide your body in one direction, using a treat as motivation. After taking a few steps in that direction, congratulate him and give him the reward. Repeat this process gradually increasing the number of steps you must take before receiving the reward. Over time, your Bichon Maltese will be able to turn completely at your command.

Another interesting trick is to "bow". To teach her this, start by holding a treat close to her nose and, while keeping her interested, slowly lower your hand to the floor. As he bends down in search of the treat, give him the command "bow". When his body approaches the ground, congratulate him and give him the reward. With practice and repetition, your Bichon Maltese will learn to perform an elegant bow on its own.

Remember that training should be fun for both your Bichon Maltese and for you. Keep sessions short and perform training exercises in a calm, distraction-free environment. Always use positive rewards, such as treats, praise and caresses, to boost their motivation and confidence.

Until this point in the chapter, you have learned some training techniques to teach your Bichon Maltese fun tricks. But this is only the beginning! In the second half of this chapter, you'll discover more surprising and exciting tricks that will allow you to continue strengthening that special bond with your beloved Bichon Maltese. So, get ready to continue exploring and having fun with your furry companion! In this second half of the chapter, we'll explore more fun tricks you can teach your Bichon Maltese to continue strengthening the bond between the two.

A very impressive trick you can teach your Bichon Maltese is to "turn around". This trick involves teaching him to turn completely in the same place. To get started, stand in front of your pet and get their attention. Then use a treat as motivation and give it the command "turn around". As you give him the command, make a circular gesture with your hand around his head. As your Bichon Maltese turns, congratulate him and reward him with the treat. Repeat this process several times, gradually increasing the speed and fluidity of the turn. With patience and practice, your furry companion will be able to turn around without the help of the treat.

Other fun tricks you can teach your Bichon Maltese include "rolling" and "jumping". To teach him to roll, start with your pet lying on his side. Then, use a candy as motivation and give it the command "roll". As you say the command, gently guide your body so that it rolls on your back to the other side. At the end of the roll, congratulate him and give him the treat as a reward. Repeat this process several times, until your Bichon Maltese can roll on its own.

To teach him to jump, use an obstacle or jump ring specifically designed for dogs. Start by placing the treat on the other side of the obstacle and give it the command "jump". Encourage your Bichon Maltese to jump over the obstacle to get the reward. Once he succeeds, congratulate him and reward him with the treat. Repeat this process several times, gradually increasing the height or difficulty of the obstacle. Always remember to consider the physical limitations of your Bichon Maltese and make sure that jumping does not pose a health risk.

As you continue to train fun tricks, don't forget to continue reinforcing the basic commands that your Bichon Maltese has previously learned. Practice "sitting" and "still" daily to help your pet maintain these fundamental skills.

Also, remember that each Maltese Bichon is unique and can have different strengths and weaknesses. Be patient and never get frustrated if your furry friend doesn't learn a trick right away. With practice, perseverance and a lot of love, you'll be able to teach her skills and tricks that will impress everyone.

In conclusion, in this chapter you have learned various training techniques to teach your Bichon Maltese fun tricks that will further strengthen your bond. From "screwing up" to "jumping", each trick will provide them with moments of fun and complicity. Continue to enjoy the learning process with your beloved Bichon Maltese, exploring new skills together and creating unforgettable memories. May they continue to share joy and love in every trick achieved!

Chapter 14: Dental Care
for the Maltese Bichon

Learn how to keep your Bichon Maltese's teeth and gums in good condition and prevent oral health problems.

Dental care is crucial to ensuring the health and well-being of your Bichon Maltese. Although we sometimes overlook this aspect, proper hygiene can prevent various oral diseases and improve the quality of life of our adorable pet. In this chapter, we'll provide you with invaluable information on how to care for your canine companion's teeth and gums.

First of all, it is important to note that Maltese Bichons are predisposed to dental problems such as plaque accumulation and tartar formation. These problems can lead to more serious periodontal diseases, causing pain, infections, and even tooth loss. Therefore, it is essential to establish a dental care routine from an early age.

One of the most effective ways to keep your Bichon Maltese's teeth clean is to brush them regularly. Daily brushing helps prevent plaque build-up and reduces tartar formation. To do this, it is advisable to use a toothbrush and toothpaste specially formulated for dogs.

When you start brushing your teeth, your Bichon Maltese may become reticent or uncomfortable. To make this experience more enjoyable, you need to gradually introduce brushing into your daily routine. You can start by stroking their lips and teeth with your finger to familiarize them with the sensation. Then, little by little, insert the toothbrush and gently massage your teeth and gums in circular motions.

Another key aspect of dental care is offering your Bichon Maltese toys and treats specifically designed to improve their oral health. There are toys that help reduce plaque build-up and strengthen the gums, such as those with special filaments or rough textures. In addition, dental treats can be an excellent option, as they stimulate chewing and naturally clean the teeth.

In addition to brushing and using dental toys, it's important to take your Bichon Maltese to the vet regularly for a professional dental checkup. Regular dental checkups make it possible to detect any oral health problem at an early stage, making it easier to treat and prevent future complications. Your veterinarian may also recommend additional treatments, such as dental cleanings or mouthwashes, depending on the specific needs of your Bichon Maltese.

In conclusion, Bichon Maltese dental care is essential to preserving their overall health and well-being. By implementing a regular brushing routine, using toys and dental treats, as well as regular visits to the vet, we can prevent dental problems and ensure a healthy and happy smile for our beloved companion. Remember, dental care not only improves the quality of life of your Bichon Maltese, but it also strengthens the bond between the two. Don't wait any longer and start providing him with the dental care he deserves! In the second half of this chapter, we'll focus on some additional recommendations for dental care for your Bichon Maltese and discuss some tips for maintaining optimal oral health.

In addition to regular brushing and incorporating toys and dental treats, there are other steps you can take to ensure excellent dental health for your pet. For example, it's important to provide him with a balanced and adequate diet to promote the health of his teeth and gums. opt for dry foods and kibble specially formulated for dental care, as they help reduce plaque build-up and tartar formation.

Also, avoid giving food and treats that are too hard or sticky, as they can damage their teeth or get stuck in their gums, which could lead to oral diseases. Remember that you are responsible for providing her with a balanced, healthy diet that takes into account her specific dental needs.

Another aspect to consider in the dental care of your Bichon Maltese is to check their mouth and teeth for any abnormalities. Watch for redness, swelling, persistent bad breath, or for signs of pain when eating or picking up toys. These symptoms could indicate the presence of underlying dental problems, such as infections or gum disease, and require immediate veterinary attention.

Remember that even with a proper dental care routine, your pet will still need a professional dental cleaning from time to time. It is advisable to schedule an annual or biannual dental cleaning with your veterinarian, who will be responsible for eliminating accumulated plaque and tartar, as well as carrying out a thorough examination of the entire oral cavity. This is a perfect opportunity to check the dental health of your Bichon Maltese and address any issues that may arise.

Finally, it's important to note that every dog is unique and may have different dental needs. Some may require more intensive dental maintenance than others because of their genetics, age, or oral health history. That's why it's crucial to be aware of changes in your Bichon Maltese's oral health and seek veterinary care in a timely manner.

In short, Bichon Maltese dental care is a fundamental part of their overall well-being. By implementing a daily brushing routine, choosing the right foods and treats, making regular visits to the vet, and taking care of any symptoms of dental problems, you're investing in the long-term health and happiness of your adorable companion. Remember that by keeping your oral health in optimal condition, you are strengthening the bond between you and your Bichon Maltese, and making sure you enjoy many years of happy smiles together. Your pet will thank you!

This concludes chapter 14 on dental care for the Maltese Bichon. We hope you found this information useful and that you feel motivated to implement a dental care routine for your beloved canine companion.

Don't hesitate to see your vet if you have any additional questions or concerns about the dental care of your Bichon Maltese. Until next time!

Chapter 15: Overcoming Separation Anxiety in the Bichon Maltese

Learn how to help your Bichon Maltese overcome separation anxiety and make him feel more relaxed when you're away.

Separation anxiety is a common concern when it comes to our adorable canine companions. The Maltese Bichon, known for its sweet and loyal personality, is no exception. While these furry friends can easily adapt to the family routine, some may experience anxiety when they are alone at home.

It's important to recognize the signs of separation anxiety in your Bichon Maltese, as this will allow us to effectively address the problem. Some of these signs can include excessive barking, whining, shattering objects, and destructive behavior, such as biting furniture or tearing pillows.

To help your Bichon Maltese overcome this anxiety, it's essential to establish a routine and create a safe and comfortable environment while you're away. Let's start by addressing some practical tips that can make a difference:

1. Gradually accustom him to being alone: Instead of abruptly disappearing from your Bichon Maltese's sight, try leaving him alone for brief moments while you're at home. As you adapt to these short intervals, gradually increase your separation time. This will help teach him that being alone doesn't always mean you're gone forever.

2. Create a safe space: Set up a specific area at home where your Bichon Maltese feels protected and comfortable. You can include their bed, toys, and familiar objects that give them a sense of familiarity and security. Make sure this area has sufficient ventilation and natural light.

3. It provides mental stimulation: Separation anxiety can also be the result of boredom. Before you head out, be sure to provide your Bichon Maltese with interactive toys or puzzles that keep him entertained and stimulate his mind. This will help distract him and keep him busy while you're away.

4. Practice quiet goodbyes: Avoid saying goodbye to your Bichon Maltese in an emotionally exaggerated way when you leave. Keep goodbyes brief and drama-free so they don't reinforce their anxiety. Upon returning home, also try to stay calm and greet him calmly after a few minutes.

5. Seek professional help if needed: If your Bichon Maltese continues to show serious signs of separation anxiety, consider seeking help from a dog behavior professional. An expert will be able to assess the situation and recommend additional techniques to help your furry friend overcome this distress.

Remember that every dog is unique, and what works for one may not be effective for another. The most important thing is to give your Bichon Maltese the support, patience and love it needs during this process of overcoming separation anxiety. Trust that you can help him feel calmer and more relaxed when you're away!

And so, with these practices and constant support, you can make a difference in the life of your Bichon Maltese. Don't forget to apply these tips gradually and with empathy, as positive change will take time. Stay hopeful as you work together to overcome separation anxiety in your adorable four-legged companion.

Remember that every dog is unique, and what works for one may not be effective for another. The most important thing is to give your Bichon Maltese the support, patience and love it needs during this process of overcoming separation anxiety. Trust that you can help him feel calmer and more relaxed when you're away!

In addition to the practical tips mentioned above, there are other strategies you can implement to help your Bichon Maltese overcome separation anxiety.

6. Train obedience commands: Performing obedience training with your Bichon Maltese can help strengthen their confidence and self-confidence. Teach him basic commands, such as sitting, staying still, or lying down, and reward him with praise and treats when he does them correctly. This will help you feel more secure when you are alone, as you will know that you can trust your abilities and you as a leader.

7. Use synthetic pheromones: Synthetic pheromones, such as diffusers or collars, can be useful for calming dogs with separation anxiety. These pheromones mimic the chemicals that dogs naturally release to communicate and convey a sense of security. Consult your veterinarian about the options available and how to use them appropriately.

8. Exercise regularly: Exercise is essential to the well-being of any dog, including the Bichon Maltese. Make sure you provide him with enough physical activity during the day, whether through walks, games, or time to run in a nearby park. A tired dog will be less prone to separation anxiety, as he will be more relaxed and calmer when you are away.

9. Establish progressive desensitization: Gradual desensitization can be an effective technique to help your Bichon Maltese overcome separation anxiety. Start by simulating short-term separation situations while you're at home, such as closing a door behind you and then reopening. As your dog gets used to it and feels calmer, you can increase the duration of the simulation.

10. Provide companionship when you're at home: Spending quality time and providing care and companionship to your Bichon Maltese when you're at home will strengthen your bond and help reduce

separation anxiety. Play with him, caress him and give him moments of intimacy. This will give him confidence and security, as he will know that he can count on you even when you are not physically present.

Remember that overcoming separation anxiety is a gradual process and it's important to be patient. If you follow these tips and give your Bichon Maltese the love and support, they need, you can make a difference in their life and help them overcome this situation.

In short, separation anxiety in the Bichon Maltese is a common challenge, but with the right approach and effective strategies, it can be overcome. Establishing a routine, creating a safe and comfortable environment, and using training and desensitization techniques will be essential in this process.

Always remember to see a professional if signs of separation anxiety persist or worsen. They can provide you with additional guidance adapted to the specific needs of your Bichon Maltese.

Keep providing the love and attention that your adorable four-legged companion needs and you'll soon see him overcome separation anxiety, achieving a stronger and happier relationship between both of you. Cheer up!

Chapter 16: The Maltese Bichon and children: a special relationship

Learn how to foster a secure and loving relationship between your Bichon Maltese and the children in the family.

Children and dogs have a special connection. Both share an overwhelming energy and an intrepid curiosity that make them ideal playmates. When it comes to raising a Bichon Maltese and having children at home, it is essential to establish a safe and loving relationship between them. In this chapter, we'll explore different ways to foster this special connection and provide a strong foundation for a lasting bond.

1. Gradual introduction: When introducing your Bichon Maltese to children, it's essential to do so gradually and under supervision. Start with brief meetings and make sure you both feel comfortable in each other's presence. Children must learn to respect the dog's space and understand their body language. As trust grows, you can gradually increase the time spent interacting with each other.

2. Teach children to be kind: It is essential that children learn to be kind and respectful to animals. Explain to them how to pet the dog properly, avoiding sudden movements or pulling its hair. Teach them to respect the rest of the Maltese Bichon and not to disturb him while he sleeps or eats. Over time, children will learn to read their dog's signs and to respect their dog's needs.

3. Constant supervision: Make sure there is always an adult monitoring any interaction between the Bichon Maltese and children.

Dogs are sensitive beings and can sometimes feel overwhelmed or uncomfortable with the actions of little ones. Being present will allow you to intervene if necessary and ensure that both the dog and the children are safe and have fun together.

4. Joint activities: Encouraging shared activities between the Bichon Maltese and children will help strengthen their bond. Organize moments of play such as throwing a soft ball for the dog to catch or teaching them simple tricks they can do together. These activities will create bonds of trust and mutual joy.

5. Teaching responsibility: As children grow, it's also important to teach them to be responsible with dog care. Involve them in tasks such as feeding the Bichon Maltese, brushing it and taking it out for a walk under supervision. This will not only teach them about the importance of animal care, but it will also strengthen their relationship and sense of responsibility to their pet.

Remember, the relationship between the Bichon Maltese and children requires time, patience and constant supervision. Only through gradual and respectful interaction can they establish a lasting bond of mutual trust. In the second half of this chapter, we will discover how the dog can become a faithful protector and playmate for children. Don't miss it! 6. Open communication: Fostering open communication between children and the Bichon Maltese is essential to strengthen their relationship. Encourage children to express how they feel in the presence of the dog and to share any concerns they may have. Also, teach them to interpret dog body language signals, such as facial language and body postures, so they can understand when the dog is happy, scared, or uncomfortable. This communication will help to avoid stressful situations for the dog and will ensure a harmonious coexistence.

7. Respect limits: It is essential to teach children to respect the limits of the Maltese Bichon. Explain to them that the dog has needs and moments of rest, just like them. Teach them not to disturb you when you are sleeping, eating, or resting in your safe place. This will ensure

that the dog feels respected and protected, and will help prevent possible aggressive behavior by the dog.

8. Positive reinforcement: Positive reinforcement is a great way to foster a positive relationship between children and the Bichon Maltese. Mistleted to the dog every time he behaves appropriately, such as when he allows children to pet him or play without showing signs of aggression. Encourage children to reward the dog with flattery, gentle petting, or even treats when it behaves well. This will reinforce good behavior and create a positive association between the dog and the children.

9. Calm attitude: Dogs are very sensitive and can quickly sense the energy of the people around them. Therefore, it is important that children learn to maintain a calm and calm attitude when they are around the Bichon Maltese. Explain that dogs may feel nervous or scared if children are yelling, running, or acting too forcefully. By teaching children to be calm, calm, and respectful, you'll help create a harmonious and safe environment for everyone.

10. Individual quality time: While it's important for children to spend time with the Bichon Maltese, it's also essential to allow the dog to have individual quality time. Children must understand that the dog needs moments of tranquility and rest, in addition to playing and interacting with them. Promote respect for the dog by encouraging children to give them space and time alone, which will strengthen their relationship and prevent the dog from feeling overwhelmed.

Remember, the relationship between the Bichon Maltese and children is special and requires time, patience and empathy. By following these tips, you'll be setting the stage for a safe and loving relationship between your Bichon Maltese and the children in your family. Don't forget that constant monitoring and open communication are key to ensuring the safety and well-being of all. Enjoy watching this beautiful connection unfold and get ready to discover in the next chapter how the Bichon Maltese can become a faithful protector and playmate for children. You can't miss it!

Chapter 17: Obedience Training for the Maltese Bichon

Learn obedience training techniques so that your Bichon Maltese becomes a well-behaved dog and responds to your commands.

The Bichon Maltese is a dog breed known for its adorable appearance and charming temperament. But while these little dogs are naturally affectionate and friendly, it's crucial to provide them with the right education to be obedient and become a faithful companion.

Obedience training is essential for any dog, and the Bichon Maltese is no exception. In addition to providing them with a solid foundation of education, this training is a great way to strengthen the bond between you and your pet. As you progress through training, you'll begin to enjoy a more harmonious and understanding relationship with your Bichon Maltese.

Before starting obedience training, it's important to understand some key aspects of the breed. Bichon Maltese are intelligent dogs that are highly motivated by positive reinforcement. This means that they will respond better to rewards, praise, and caresses, rather than punishment or harsh methods. Creating a positive and motivating learning environment for them is essential.

One of the first lessons you should teach your Bichon Maltese is the basic command of "sitting". This is a fundamental behavior that allows them to remain calm in different situations and makes it easier to control them. To teach them this command, you will simply need patience, a little time and some tasty treats.

Start by showing your Bichon Maltese a treat and holding it over his nose. Then slowly lift the treat upward while clearly pronouncing the word "sitting". This will motivate your dog to tilt his head back and sit naturally. The moment he sits down, congratulate him and reward him with the treat.

Remember to repeat this exercise several times, but don't prolong each training session too long. Bichon Maltese have shorter attention spans because of their size and energy. Keep training sessions short, but frequent, to avoid getting bored or distracted.

Once your Bichon Maltese has assimilated the "sitting" command, you can move to the next level and teach him the "still" command. This is a fundamental step to strengthen their capacity for self-discipline and to control their behavior in different situations.

To train the "still" command, start with your dog sitting in front of you. Then slowly reach out your hand to him with your palm down and clearly pronounce the word "still". Make sure your tone of voice is firm but friendly. If your Bichon Maltese stays still for a few seconds, congratulate him and reward him with a treat.

These are just a few examples of obedience training techniques you can use with your Bichon Maltese. With patience, consistency and positive reinforcement, your dog will be able to learn a wide variety of commands and behaviors that will make him a well-behaved and obedient companion.

One of the key aspects of obedience training for the Maltese Bichon is to teach them to walk on a leash in a calm and controlled manner. This is especially important because of the small size of this dog breed, as they tend to be more prone to stretching the leash or acting impulsively during walks.

To begin teaching your Bichon Maltese to walk properly on a leash, it is recommended to use a harness instead of a collar. The harness will distribute the pressure of the leash more evenly and prevent damage to your pet's neck.

Start by attaching the harness to your Bichon Maltese and place the strap on the harness ring. Keep the leash short but not tense, and start walking with your dog. If your Bichon Maltese pulls on the leash, stop and wait for it to calm down before continuing to walk.

As you walk, it's important to remember to be the leader of the ride. Maintain a firm stance and show confidence with every step you take. This will help to convey to your Bichon Maltese that you are in control and that he must follow you.

When walking your Bichon Maltese, avoid sudden pulls on the strap. Instead, use commands like "here" or "next to me" to tell him that you want him to walk beside you. If your dog obeys you, congratulate him and reward him with a tasty treat.

In addition to training during the walk, it is important to remember that patience and consistency are essential in the obedience training process for the Maltese Bichon. Don't expect immediate results and don't be discouraged if your dog doesn't respond immediately to your commands. Remember that every dog learns at their own pace and it may be necessary to modify training techniques to adapt to the individual needs of your Bichon Maltese.

In short, obedience training for the Maltese Bichon is essential for your pet to become a well-behaved and obedient dog. Through techniques based on positive reinforcement, such as the use of treats and praise, you can teach him basic commands such as "sitting" and "still". Also, during walks, it's important to establish effective communication with your Bichon Maltese so that he learns to walk with you without stretching his leash. Always remember to be patient, to be consistent, and to give your dog the love and care it deserves.

Chapter 18: The Bichon Maltese as a competition dog

Discover the innate abilities and aptitudes of the Maltese Bichon and how to prepare it to compete in different canine disciplines.

The Bichon Maltese, known for its elegance and friendly character, not only stands out as an exceptional companion dog, but has also proven to be a true athlete in the world of canine competition. Despite its delicate appearance, this small dog has a series of innate abilities and aptitudes that allow it to excel in different disciplines.

First of all, the Bichon Maltese shows great physical agility, making it an ideal dog to compete in agility tests. Its compact size and lightness allow it to move quickly and quickly through the different obstacles that arise in this type of competition. In addition, his curious spirit and intelligence help him to quickly learn the routines and strategies necessary to overcome the challenges of these tests.

Another outstanding ability of the Maltese Bichon is its ability to train in obedience. This dog is highly responsive to commands and enjoys learning. Their obedient attitude and desire to please their owners make them a popular choice in obedience competitions. The Bichon Maltese can perform a wide variety of commands, from the most basic to the most complex, thus demonstrating its intelligence and willingness to exceed expectations.

In addition to its agility and obedience, the Maltese Bichon has also demonstrated talent in exhibition competitions. Its elegant white coat and refined shape make it an ideal dog to participate in canine beauty contests. This little dog has a charming presence and knows how to stand out on stage, capturing the attention of the judges and the public. His natural grace and confidence make him a formidable contender in these types of events.

To prepare a Bichon Maltese to compete in different disciplines, it's important to start from an early age. Constant training and proper socialization are critical to unlocking your full potential. It is essential to establish a strong foundation in obedience and to strengthen it as the dog grows. In addition, it is advisable to seek the guidance of specialized trainers who can help you develop the specific skills required for each discipline in which you want to compete.

In short, the Bichon Maltese is much more than a companion dog, it has innate abilities and aptitudes that make it a true competitor in the world of canine competition. Their agility, obedience and charming presence make them stand out in disciplines such as agility, obedience and canine beauty contests. If you're looking for a faithful and loving companion who can also shine in competitions, the Bichon Maltese is the perfect choice.

At the end of this first half of the chapter, much remains to be discovered about the Bichon Maltese as a competition dog. In the second half of this chapter, we'll explore your specific training for each discipline, as well as practical tips to prepare you mentally and physically before taking on the competitions. Don't miss the exciting continuation of this story, where we'll reveal the secrets to turning your Bichon Maltese into a true champion. As we continue to explore the abilities of the Maltese Bichon as a competition dog, it is crucial to understand the importance of its specific training for each discipline. While this little dog is naturally talented and agile, it takes time and effort to shape his skills and maximize his potential. Next, I'll provide you with practical tips to mentally and physically prepare your Bichon Maltese before taking on the competitions.

First of all, agility training is a discipline in which the Bichon Maltese can shine. Before you start working on obstacles and agility routines, it's essential to make sure your dog has a solid foundation in basic obedience. This includes commands such as sitting down, staying still, and coming when called. These commands are essential to maintaining control of your dog during agility tests.

Once your Bichon Maltese has a solid foundation of obedience, you can begin to introduce the obstacles of agility. Some of the common elements in these tests include jumps, tunnels, walkways, and rockers. Be sure to teach your dog how to face each obstacle individually, using positive reinforcement and rewards as rewards.

As your Bichon Maltese becomes more familiar with the different obstacles, you can start working on agility routines. These routines usually include a variety of obstacles in a specific order, and it's important that your dog learns to perform them with fluidity and precision. Use positive reinforcement and verbal markings to tell your dog what obstacle to overcome next.

When it comes to obedience training, it's crucial that your Bichon Maltese knows how to respond quickly to your commands. In addition to basic commands such as sitting and staying still, it's important to teach your dog more specific commands depending on the obedience discipline you want to compete in.

For example, if you plan to participate in advanced obedience competitions, you'll need to teach your dog commands such as "jump", "cover" and "bring". Advanced obedience classes can be extremely useful for refining these commands and for learning more advanced training techniques.

Last but not least, if you want your Bichon Maltese to participate in dog beauty contests, you must pay special attention to their care and grooming. This dog is known for its beautiful white fur, which must be kept clean and free of tangles. Also, make sure your haircut is suitable for canine beauty competitions.

To achieve this, consider taking your dog to a specialized dog groomer who has experience preparing dogs for these types of events. Daily brushing is essential to keep your Bichon Maltese's coat in good condition, and don't forget to pay attention to their nails, teeth and ears to ensure they are always clean and healthy.

In conclusion, preparing your Bichon Maltese to compete in different canine disciplines requires time, dedication and specific training. His agility, obedience and charming presence are qualities that can be shaped and honed to become a true champion. Always remember to use positive reinforcement, be patient, and provide your dog with a safe and supportive environment. Good luck in your future competitions with your faithful companion Bichon Maltese!

Chapter 19: The special care of a Maltese Bichon in old age

Old age is a time of life full of change and challenges for everyone, including our beloved pets. When our faithful companion, the Bichon Maltese, reaches old age, he requires special care to guarantee him a full and happy life.

During this stage of our Bichon Maltese's life, their energy and vitality may gradually decrease. It is essential to be aware of physical and behavioral changes that may occur and to adapt our care accordingly.

One of the main precautions we must take into account is diet. In old age, Bichons Maltese may experience changes in their appetite and metabolism. They may prefer softer, easier to digest foods. A balanced diet, rich in nutrients and adapted to your specific needs, is essential to maintaining your health and well-being.

In addition to food, it is essential to pay attention to the physical activity of our Bichon Maltese in old age. While it's normal for their energy and ability to exercise to decrease, it's important to continue to stimulate them physically through milder activities, such as short walks and quiet games. This will help them stay in shape and prevent being overweight, which can bring with it a number of health problems.

Another crucial aspect of caring for an elderly Maltese Bichon is regular medical care. Visits to the veterinarian should take place more frequently, to detect possible health problems and to take preventive or treatment measures in time. In addition, regular dental checkups are essential, as oral health can deteriorate over the years.

At this stage in the life of our adorable companion, we must pay special attention to their comfort and well-being. Providing you with a comfortable place to rest, with an adequate bed and protected from drafts, is key to making you feel safe and relaxed. It is also important to adapt your environment to your needs, avoiding obstacles or steps that could hinder your mobility.

Love and emotional attention are also essential in caring for a Maltese Bichon in old age. As they age, they may experience changes in their behavior, such as seeking affection or moments of apathy. Dedicate quality time, pampering and positive reinforcement to strengthen their bond and provide them with the emotional security they need.

In short, old age is a stage in which our Bichon Maltese needs special care to ensure a full and happy life. From a balanced diet adapted to their needs, adequate physical activity, regular medical care and a comfortable environment, to the love and emotional attention they deserve, all these aspects are essential to ensure their well-being at this stage of life. Now that we understand the essential care in old age for our beloved Bichon Maltese, it's time to delve into the specific challenges that may arise and the techniques to overcome them. One of the specific challenges that can arise in the old age of a Bichon Maltese is the onset of age-related diseases and medical conditions. It's important to be alert to any signs of discomfort or changes in your behavior, as they could indicate the presence of health problems.

One of the most common problems in older dogs is arthritis, a degenerative joint disease that can cause pain and discomfort. If you notice your Bichon Maltese having trouble moving, limping, or showing joint stiffness, it's crucial to take him to the vet for a proper diagnosis. Your veterinarian may prescribe medications or treatments to relieve pain and improve your pet's quality of life.

In addition to arthritis, Bichons Maltese can also be prone to eye problems in old age. Cataracts, macular degeneration and glaucoma are some of the eye conditions that can affect these older dogs. It's important to have regular eye exams and follow your veterinarian's recommendations to prevent or treat any eye problems.

Hearing loss is also common in older dogs, including Maltese dogs. If you notice that your pet doesn't respond when you call them, that they get scared easily, or that they seem disoriented, they may have trouble hearing. In these cases, it's important to be patient and use visual cues to communicate with your dog. Avoid loud sounds and maintain a calm environment to help you feel safe.

Another challenge that can arise in the old age of a Bichon Maltese is urinary incontinence. As in humans, bladder muscles can weaken with age, leading to leaks or accidents. If you notice that your pet is having trouble controlling urination, it's important to see your veterinarian to rule out any underlying medical problems and for guidance on how to manage incontinence.

To provide your Bichon Maltese with adequate care in their old age, it's essential to adapt their environment to their changing needs. You can set up ramps or ladders to facilitate their access to elevated places, make sure there are no dangerous objects within reach, and avoid sudden changes in routine that could cause stress or anxiety.

Remember that old age is a stage in which our Bichon Maltese needs special attention and constant love. Dedicate quality time to your pet, pet them gently, talk to them lovingly and provide positive reinforcement. Maintain a calm and comfortable environment so that he can enjoy his well-deserved rest, and remember that your love and care are essential to guarantee him a full and happy life at this stage of his life.

With these tips and special care, you can give your aging Bichon Maltese the attention it deserves and help it to enjoy its old age in the best possible way. Don't forget that your faithful companion will always be grateful for the love and dedication you give him, and his presence in your life will always be an inexhaustible source of joy and companionship.

Chapter 20: The Maltese Bichon as another member of the family

We will reflect on the importance of the Bichon Maltese as another member of the family and how his unconditional love can enrich our lives.

In life, there are few things that can match the selfless love and loyalty of a dog. When we think of our families, it's common to imagine our loved ones, the ones who share our daily lives. However, what happens when we consider our pets within this circle?

Known for its beauty and charming personality, the Bichon Maltese has become one of the most faithful and loving companions anyone could have. Their small size and affable character make them quickly earn a special place in the hearts of their owners. But beyond its appearance and charm, the Maltese Bichon is capable of being a valuable and unique member of the family.

One of the most outstanding qualities of the Maltese Bichon is its ability to provide unconditional love. These adorable four-legged stuffed animals are willing to give everything for their loved ones. Their loyalty is undeniable and their devotion to their owners is extraordinary. When we get home after a long day at work, it's comforting to be greeted by that line that keeps moving and those little eyes full of happiness. The Maltese Bichon instantly restores joy and makes us feel loved and valued.

In addition to their selfless love, the Bichon Maltese can also enrich our lives in many other ways. Their constant presence can bring a sense of companionship and comfort. For those who live alone or have a lonely routine, having a Bichon Maltese as part of the family can make a big difference. Their energy and enthusiasm infect everyone around them, reminding us that life is full of joyful and fun moments.

Not only do they give us positive emotions, but they can also help us stay active. Maltese Bichons are quite energetic and enjoy activities such as walks, games and training. Engaging in these activities with our pets not only helps us to stay physically active, but it also strengthens the bond we share with them. In addition, these shared moments allow us to release accumulated stress and enjoy the gratification of seeing each other happy and satisfied.

In short, the Bichon Maltese is much more than just a pet, it becomes a beloved member of the family. His unconditional love and ability to brighten and enrich our lives are unparalleled. In the next chapter, we'll further explore how the presence of the Bichon Maltese can influence our family relationships and how we can care for and maintain their well-being. Get ready to discover new ways to strengthen your bond with this charming dog breed.

The love and bond that develops between a Maltese Bichon and their family are extremely important. Not only does this little dog provide unconditional love, but it can also positively influence our family relationships and our overall well-being.

One of the highlights of having a Bichon Maltese as a family member is their ability to bring people together. These adorable four-legged stuffed animals can break barriers and bring people of different ages and backgrounds together. It's amazing how a little dog can make everyone feel closer and more connected. The moments shared with the Bichon Maltese, such as family walks or play sessions, create bonds between parents and children, siblings and grandparents. This constant interaction with a pet helps strengthen family ties and encourages communication and teamwork.

In addition, the Bichon Maltese also has the power to be a great source of comfort. In times of stress or difficulty, having our furry friend close by can make a big difference. Their simple presence can ease anxiety and provide emotional support. Caressing their soft fur can be comforting and calm your nerves. Maltese dogs have an innate ability to read our emotions and provide us with comfort when we need it most.

Another way in which the Bichon Maltese can enrich our lives is by teaching responsibility. Keeping a dog at home involves a series of duties and responsibilities that must be fulfilled. Including children in the daily care of the Bichon Maltese can be an excellent opportunity to teach them the importance of caring for and being responsible for another living being. By assigning tasks such as feeding the dog, brushing it or taking it for a walk, children are fostered a sense of responsibility and care for other living beings.

Caring for a Maltese Bichon can also be beneficial to our health and well-being. These dogs are known for their intuition when it comes to human emotions. They can detect subtle changes in our mood and react in ways that bring us comfort or joy. Their constant presence can reduce stress and promote an overall sense of well-being.

In conclusion, having a Bichon Maltese as a member of the family goes beyond having a simple pet. Their unconditional love, their ability to bring people together and their positive influence on our family relationships are aspects that cannot be underestimated. Through its constant companionship, the Bichon Maltese can bring us joy, comfort and teach us important lessons in responsibility. We must always remember the immense value that our pets have in our lives.

Next time, we'll explore how to care for and maintain the well-being of our Bichon Maltese, giving them everything they need to be happy and healthy. Don't miss the tips and advice in the next chapter!

Disclaimer of Liability

This book has been created with the purpose of providing general information about dogs of the Bichon Maltese breed. Although considerable effort has been made to ensure that the information provided is accurate and up to date, the author and publisher cannot guarantee the complete accuracy of all content.

Descriptions of the characteristics, behavior, care and other aspects related to Maltese Bichons are generalizations and may not apply to every individual of the breed. Every dog is unique and can vary in their temperament, health, and behavior.

The advice and recommendations given in this book are indicative and should not be considered as a substitute for professional veterinary advice. It is always recommended to consult a qualified veterinarian for any concerns related to the health and well-being of your pet.

The author and publisher are not responsible for the results obtained by applying the techniques or advice mentioned in this book. The responsibility for the proper care and management of any pet lies entirely with the animal's owner.

The cases and anecdotes mentioned in the book are for illustrative purposes and should not be interpreted as specific situations that all Maltese Bichons owners will experience.

This book is not sponsored or endorsed by any organization or brand related to Maltese Bichon or any other type of dog. The opinions expressed are those of the author and do not necessarily reflect those of any entity related to dog breeds.

Don't miss out!

Visit the website below and you can sign up to receive emails whenever Gonzalo Estrada publishes a new book. There's no charge and no obligation.

https://books2read.com/r/B-A-OZBBB-EKJZC

BOOKS2READ

Connecting independent readers to independent writers.

Did you love *The Maltese Bichon*? Then you should read *The ABC of Educating Your Pet*[1] by Gonzalo Estrada!

Unlock the secrets to a well-behaved pet with "The ABC of Educating Your Pet" by Gonzalo Estrada. This comprehensive guide takes you through the essential steps of training your furry friend in a compassionate and violence-free manner. From creating a conducive environment to understanding the nuances of pet psychology, each chapter is a step towards a deeper bond between you and your pet.

Learn the art of positive education as you establish routines, teach proper bathroom habits, and use positive reinforcement to shape behavior. Navigate common training challenges with patience and consistency, and discover how to maintain calm in stressful situations. With insights on socialization, hygiene, and health, this book is your

---

1. https://books2read.com/u/mq9682

2. https://books2read.com/u/mq9682

all-in-one resource for fostering a loving and respectful relationship with your pet.

Whether you're dealing with a fearful pup or an anxious feline, "The ABC of Educating Your Pet" provides practical advice and proven techniques to ensure your pet's well-being and happiness. Embrace the role of a responsible pet owner and enjoy the journey of nurturing a well-trained companion.

Also by Gonzalo Estrada

Self Healing
Visualiza tu Éxito
Cultivando Líderes
Afirmaciones y Empoderamiento
Semillas de Cambio
Cómo convertir TikTok en una máquina de hacer dinero
Cómo hacer dinero con Pinterest
Cómo hacer un ensayo
Cómo Pedir un Aumento de Sueldo
Currículo Poderoso
Entrenamiento sin Violencia
Entrevista Laboral
Gana Dinero con X (Twitter)
Ganar Masa Muscular
Volver a Empezar; el arte de reinventarse
Analiza Resuelve Ejecuta
Aromatherapy, The natural path to your pet´s well being
Holistic Feeding
The ABC of Educating Your Pet
The Art of Cosmic Connection
The Art of Feng Shui applied to your Pets
From Scarcity to Abundance
The English Bulldog in The Family
The French Bulldog
Therapeutic Massages for Pets

Pets and Crystal Therapy
The Maltese Bichon

About the Author

Gonzalo Estrada es un autor prolífico y reconocido, cuyos libros abarcan temas que apasionan a la humanidad. Con una presencia destacada en los principales medios tanto físicos como en línea, Estrada ha dejado una marca significativa en la literatura contemporánea. Sus obras, de gran trascendencia en plataformas como Amazon, Barnes & Noble y muchas otras, reflejan su profundo conocimiento y pasión por los temas que aborda. Desde el poder transformador de la gratitud hasta la singular personalidad del Bulldog Francés, Estrada ha demostrado ser un escritor versátil y cautivador que ha sabido conectar con lectores de todas partes del mundo.